W9-CSV-300

1992

Merry Christmas Luke

Here's to some
"Space-free!"

Love,
Aunt Karen
+ Uncle Tom

SPACE-CRAFTING
Invent Your Own Flying Spaceships

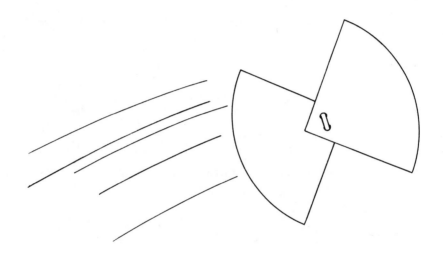

Mary Blocksma & Dewey Blocksma

illustrated by Art Seiden

Simon and Schuster Books for Young Readers
Published by Simon & Schuster Inc.
New York

Simon and Schuster Books for Young Readers
Simon & Schuster Building
Rockefeller Center
1230 Avenue of the Americas
New York, New York 10020

Text copyright © 1986 by Mary Blocksma
and Dewey Blocksma
Illustrated copyright © 1986 Art Seiden

All rights reserved
including the right of reproduction
in whole or in part in any form.
Published by the Simon & Schuster Juvenile Division
SIMON AND SCHUSTER BOOKS FOR YOUNG READERS
is a trademark of Simon & Schuster Inc.

Designed by Constance Ftera
Manufactured in the United States of America

10   9   8   7   6   5   4   3   2

Library of Congress Cataloging in Publication Data

Blocksma, Mary.
    Space-crafting.

    Summary: Presents basic information for transforming
household materials into futuristic crafts.
    1. Space vehicles—Models—Juvenile literature.
[1. Space vehicles—Models.   2. Handicraft]
I. Blocksma, Dewey.   II. Seiden, Art, Ill.   III. Title.
TL844.B58   1986   629.40'228   86-9422
ISBN 0-671-66300-3

To
Sandy
and
aerospace dreamers
everywhere

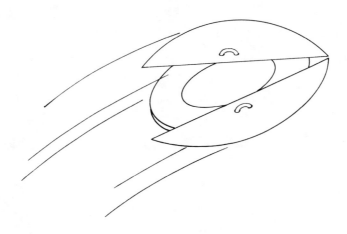

CONTENTS

HOW TO SPACE-CRAFT

You really can invent flying spaceships! It's easy! First, build your own spaceship kit and make some of the 24 models in this book. Then jazz up your spaceships or put the parts together in new ways.

To fly your spaceships, fling them flat like a Frisbee. Use wrist action to put some spin on them. Some of your spaceships may be too big to fly gracefully, but most will flash through the air like bees.

Your spaceships will look impressive, because they're made from or decorated with dazzling, color-crazy *plastic!* Plastic is fantastic space-age stuff—it's tough, bright, easy to work with, and very often free.

To get started, gather the following simple tools and materials, and learn a few tricks about working with plastic.

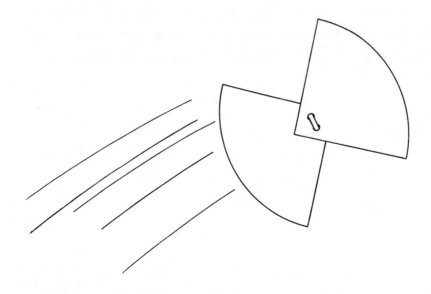

WHAT YOU NEED

TOOLS

Three tools are all you need:
a ball-point pen or permanent marker for writing on plastic
a paper punch
a pair of strong scissors.

MATERIALS

Most of the spaceships in this book are made from household stuff—plastic straws, plastic wrap, cardboard cartons, and the like. The other materials are easy to find.

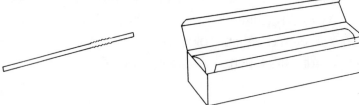

Plastic lids

Use only thick, bendable plastic. (Fast food lids don't work!) Brightly colored plastic lids come on many cans of nuts, catfood, coffee, soup mixes, and other foods. Plain lids from margarine tubs and many other containers work too.

Plastic picnicware

Find cups—the squat, cone-shaped ones with flat bottoms are nice—
as well as bowls or plates at most supermarkets. Get the brightest
colors you can find. Cardboard picnicware works, too, although it
isn't as bright.

Vinyl tubing

For a Rim Spinner, buy about 2 feet of *soft* aquarium tubing (no fatter
than your little finger) at most hardware stores.

For a Hoopship, buy about 3½ feet of *stiff*, fat vinyl tubing (bigger
around than your thumb) in the plumbing department of most
hardware stores.

Plastic tape

Use only plastic tape—insulating tape, electrical tape, or duct tape—
which often comes in bright colors. Masking tape works, but it isn't
so handsome.

Glue

Stick all sorts of wonderful things to your spaceships with white glue or rubber cement.

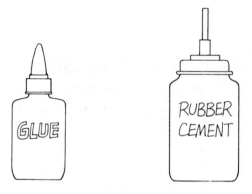

DECORATIONS

Decorating may be the best part of making spaceships. To get started, check out the spaceship designs on the cover of this book. Then do your own.

1. *Stick things to it!* For 3-D excitement, stick all sorts of things to your spaceships with tape, white glue, or rubber cement. Give glue plenty of time to dry. Here are some things to stick on:

   bright plastic caps from used-up cosmetics, felt pens, and empty bottles
   hangers from new socks

thread spools
paper clips
picnicware cups and bowls
pipe cleaners (great antennae)
and many, many more

2. *Tape it!* Bright, inexpensive plastic tape makes great designs.

3. *Glue or paint designs on it!*
   Paint: You can paint anything you like—spirals, bands of color, or designs. Not all paints or other coloring stuff will stick to plastic, though. Here are some kinds that will. (Be sure to let the paint dry.)

acrylic paints   crayons
permanent felt markers   model paint
permanent inks   latex wall or house paint
(Poster paint is all right, but it washes off or chips.)

YIPES!!! Colors that stick to plastic won't wash out of your clothes! Be careful when you use them.

Stick-on designs: Cut designs—triangles with rounded corners and doughnut shapes cut into pieces are especially space-y—and stick them on with white glue or rubber cement. (For a racy look, punch a hole in a shape. Then punch another hole in the spaceship. Stick the bending end of a plastic straw through both holes.) For other outstanding results, use some of these great materials:

stickers (bright dots are classy)   aluminum foil
foil gift wrap   candy and gum wrappers
glitter (paint designs with rubber cement and sprinkle glitter on top)
bright plastic see-through theme covers (inexpensive at dime stores)
plastic picnicware scraps (great for nose pieces and rocket engines)

OR-BITS

Put a few plastic parts together with plastic tabs, and you have yourself an Or-Bit! Just make whatever Or-Bit parts you need (see pages 12 to 18 for how to make Or-Bit parts). Then follow the steps to put them together. Later, you can take your Or-Bit apart to make another one, or make some new parts and tabs. Before long you'll be inventing your own Or-Bit designs!

Hints for making great Or-Bits

1. Remember that the top of the lid is the top of the Or-Bit.
2. If you use large lids or add many parts, anchor the tabs underneath with plastic tape. Tab strips alone will hold small Or-Bits.
3. When directions call for more than one of something, make them all the same size.

OR-BIT PARTS

You can make a kit of these parts by making them all at the same time, or make the ones you need for each Or-Bit as you go along. You'll need all three tools—scissors, paper punch, and pen.

Materials: plastic lids

Or-Bit Parts

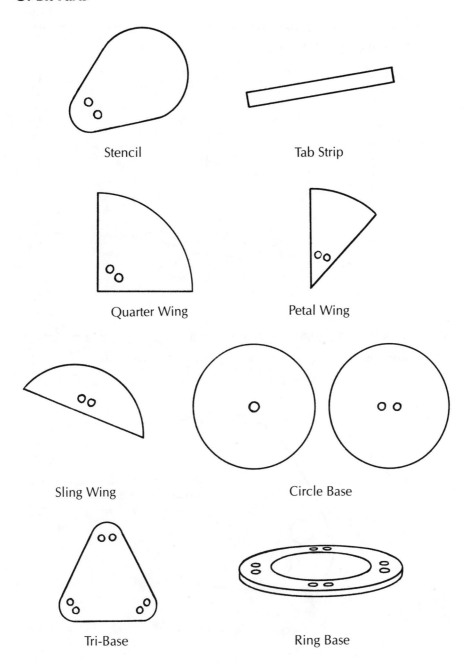

Stencil

Tab Strip

Quarter Wing

Petal Wing

Sling Wing

Circle Base

Tri-Base

Ring Base

Stencil

The stencil helps you make sure all the holes you make line up, so the pieces fit together. It's important!

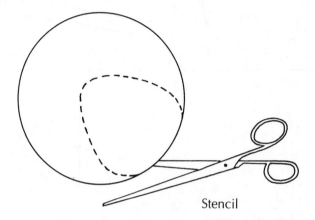

Stencil

Cut a stencil from a plastic lid—make it the same size as the "Actual Size" drawing. Use a paper punch to make the holes.

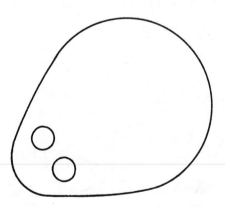

Stencil (Actual Size)

Tab Strips

1. Cut a lid in half. Then cut a strip off a straight edge. Make the strip just wide enough to go through the holes in your stencil.

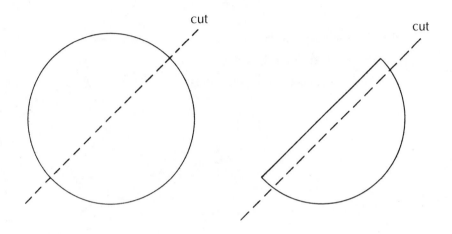

2. Cut off the rims. Then cut the strip to make pieces about as long as your thumb.

3. Make lots of tab strips. Just keep cutting from the straight edges of the lid. Don't make your tab strips too thin. Loose tab strips won't hold Or-Bits together in the air.

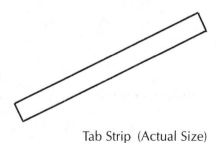

Tab Strip (Actual Size)

Using the Stencil and Tab Strips

To make sure all your Or-Bit parts fit together, use the stencil every time you make holes. Then use a tab strip to put the parts together. Here's how:

1. Hold the holes in the stencil over any piece where it needs holes. Mark the holes with a ball-point pen.

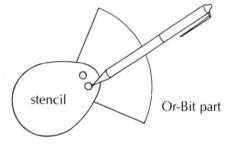

stencil

Or-Bit part

2. Punch out the holes.

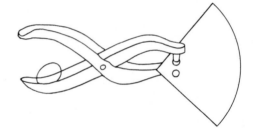

3. Put two pieces together so the holes match up.

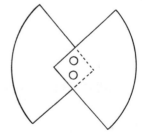

4. Stick a tab strip end through each hole.

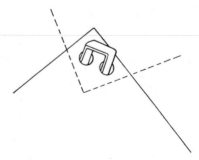

Quarter Wings

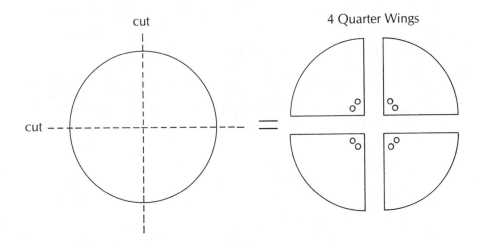

cut

4 Quarter Wings

1. Cut a lid in half. Then cut each piece in half again.

2. Use the stencil to mark holes in each pointed end. Punch out the holes.

Petal Wings

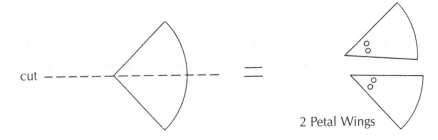

cut

2 Petal Wings

1. Cut a Quarter Wing in half before punching holes in it.

2. Use the stencil to mark holes in each pointed end. Punch out the holes.

Sling Wings and Tri-Base

1. Draw a triangle on a lid. Leaving the rim on, make each point touch an edge. Cut out the triangle. The three small parts are Sling Wings. The middle is the Tri-Base.

2. Use the stencil and a pen to make holes in the middle of each Sling Wing and at each point of the Tri-Base. Punch out the holes. Round off the sharp corners of the Tri-Base with the scissors.

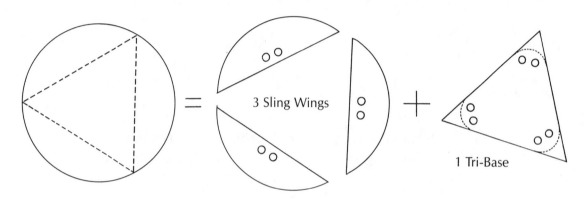

3 Sling Wings

1 Tri-Base

Ring Base and Circle Base

1. Cut a circle from the middle of a lid. Don't cut through the outside ring!

2. Use stencil and pen to mark holes across from each other on the ring (see drawing of Ring Base) and in the middle of the circle. Punch the holes.

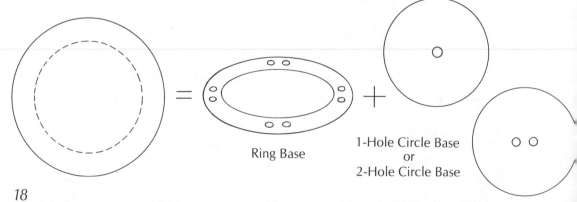

Ring Base

1-Hole Circle Base
or
2-Hole Circle Base

MACH MITE

Here's a quickie to get you started—and does it ever fly! Use small lids for these Or-Bit parts—small Mach Mites fly better than big ones.

Or-Bit parts:

1 tab strip   2 quarter wings

1. Match up the holes in the quarter wings.

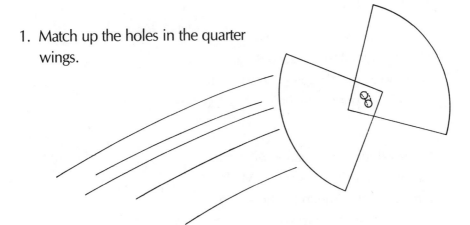

2. Put one end of the tab strip through each hole.

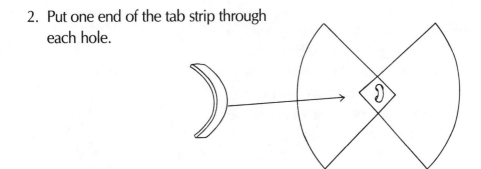

TRI-MITE

Adding a third wing just takes a little stencil magic.

Or-Bit parts:

2 tab strips   3 quarter wings   stencil

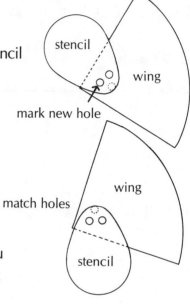

1. Match up one hole in the stencil with one quarter wing hole. Put the second stencil hole at the point. Mark the hole.

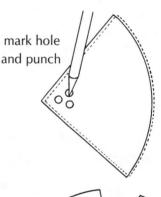

2. Use the stencil to make sure the wing holes match up every way you set it. Then punch the hole.

3. Lay the three-hole quarter wing on top of another quarter wing. Mark the third hole. Punch the hole. Do this again for the third wing.

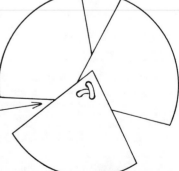

4. Set the three quarter wings with points together so the holes match up—you should see three holes. Put each tab strip through any two holes. (One of the holes holds two tab strip ends.)

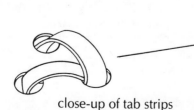

close-up of tab strips

PETAL SHIP

The ridges in one small piece of straw hold all these parts together!

Or-Bit parts: 4 petal wings   1 circle base with 1 hole

Other materials: 1 plastic elbow straw

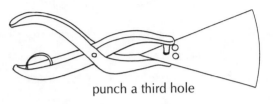

1. Punch a third hole at the point of each petal wing.

punch a third hole

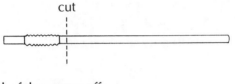

cut

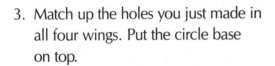

2. Cut the bending end of the straw off. Discard the straight piece.

3. Match up the holes you just made in all four wings. Put the circle base on top.

4. Pull the ridged piece of straw through the hole to the middle of the bend—pull hard! (If you have trouble getting the straw through the hole, pinch one end of the straw twice.)

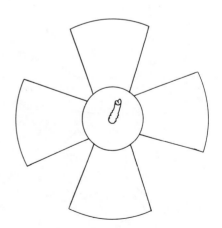

NIP SHIP

Now things are really getting space-y!

Or-Bit parts: 1 quarter wing   1 2-hole circle base   stencil
                   1 sling wing   1 tab strip

Other materials: 1 plastic lid

1. Cut a small triangle from the plastic lid for a nose piece. Use the stencil to make two holes at its base.

3. Use the drawing to help you stack up the pieces, matching the holes. Put the tab strip through the holes.

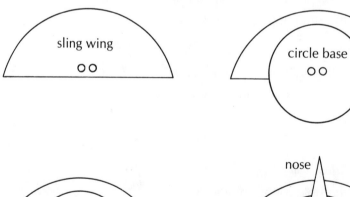

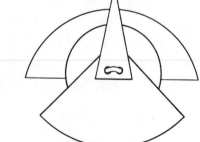

TRI-FLY

For a trim model, use parts made of small lids—or experiment and mix big parts with small.

Or-Bit parts: 1 quarter wing 2 sling wings
1 tri-base 3 tab strips

Nifty extras: 1 plastic elbow straw; bright scraps of plastic lids or plates

1. Use tab strips to attach each sling wing to a point of the tri-base.

2. Use the last tab strip to attach the quarter wing to the last tri-base point.

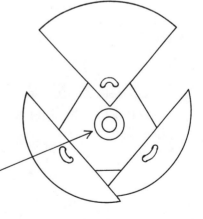

To decorate your Tri-Fly, stick the bending end of a straw through the center hole. It will hold bright circles cut from plastic scraps.

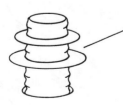

RING RACER

Some plastic lids will fly even if you don't do anything to them. Most of them fly better, though, if you cut the middle out. Just make the ring base on page 18. Later, make it into something fancy—like a Sprinter!

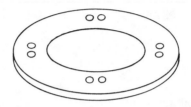

SPRINTER

This is more like it!

Or-Bit parts: 2 quarter wings   2 sling wings   1 ring base
                 5 tab strips   stencil

Other materials: plastic lid scrap

1. Use the stencil to mark two sets of new holes on the ring base (see drawing).

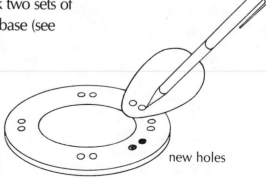

new holes

2. Use a tab strip to attach a sling wing to each new set of holes.

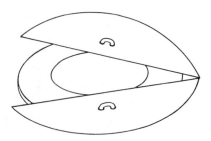

3. Attach the quarter wings between the sling wings with tab strips, as in the drawing.

4. Cut a nose piece from a plastic scrap.

5. Using the stencil, make holes in the base of the nose piece. Make another set of holes in the middle of the curved part of one quarter wing.

6. Attach the nose to the quarter wing with a tab strip.

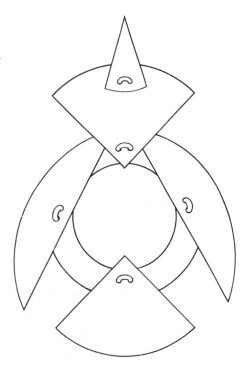

SPINNERATOR

Here's a secret: if you're lucky, your plastic picnicware bowls will snap right into one of your larger lids. You won't even need tape.

Or-Bit parts: 1 large ring base

Other Materials: 1 picnicware bowl (plastic or cardboard)
plastic tape

1. Cut the rim off the bowl, little by little, until it fits upside down into the top of the ring base. (You can cut a slit in the bowl and overlap the edges, holding them with tape, to make it fit.)

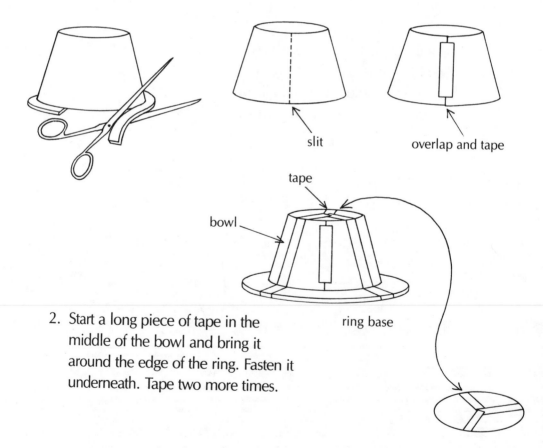

slit

overlap and tape

tape

bowl

ring base

2. Start a long piece of tape in the middle of the bowl and bring it around the edge of the ring. Fasten it underneath. Tape two more times.

SPINNERATOR 2

Jazz up a Spinnerator, and you might get something like this!

Or-Bit parts: 1 large ring base   3 quarter wings   3 tab strips

Materials: 1 picnicware bowl (plastic or cardboard)
              plastic tape

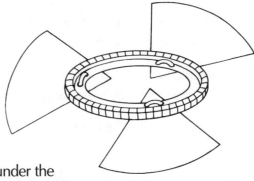

1. Attach the quarter wings under the
   ring base with tab strips, as shown
   in the drawing. (Use stencil to make
   new holes in the base if you need to.)

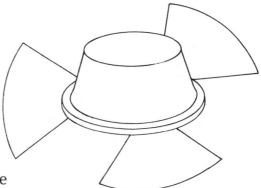

2. Follow instructions for the
   Spinnerator (page 26), using this
   jazzed-up ring base.

X-PLORER

Take on the universe with this starship model!

Or-Bit parts: 4 quarter wings   4 tab strips   stencil

Other materials: 1 large plastic lid   1 cone-shaped plastic cup

1. Set the cup upside down in the middle of the plastic lid. Trace around the cup. Cut just inside the line (don't cut through the ring).

2. Using the stencil, punch four sets of holes in the ring, as in the drawing.

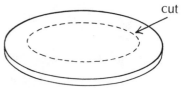

cut

3. Use tab strips to attach the quarter wings under the ring at the holes.

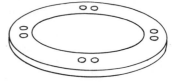

4. Push the cup up from the bottom through the big center hole. Tape the cup to the ring underneath.

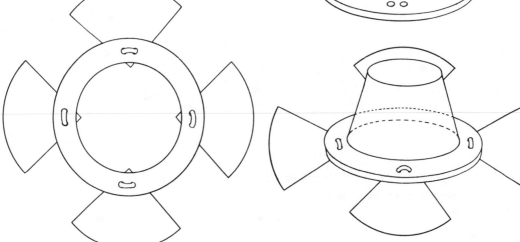

ASTRONAUT

If you can see through your X-Plorer cockpit, make a pilot to ride inside.

Or-Bit parts: 2 tab strips   stencil

Materials: 1 large lid (same size as X-Plorer's)
tape
pilot (use small toy or draw
a face on a plastic
bottle cap)
cone-shaped cup to trace
around

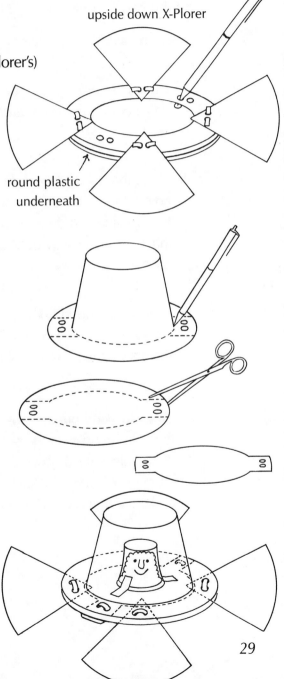

upside down X-Plorer

round plastic
underneath

1. Using the stencil, punch two sets of holes in the X-Plorer ring base, as in the drawing.

2. Cut the rim off the plastic lid. Hold the round piece under the X-Plorer ring. Mark the two new sets of holes. Punch them.

3. Set a spare cone cup in the middle of the plastic round and trace around it. Draw tabs around the holes, as in the drawing. Cut out circle to include the tabs.

4. Tape or glue the pilot onto the circle. Use two tab strips to fasten the piece underneath the X-Plorer.

CUPNIK

This little number is a sweet flyer.

Or-Bit parts: 1 ring base   2 tab strips   stencil

Other materials: 1 plastic or paper cup (but not styrofoam)

1. Draw lines on the cup, dividing it in half around the middle *and* over the bottom.

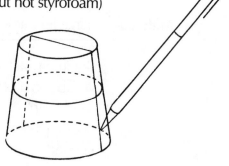

2. Using the stencil, punch two sets of holes close to the edge of the cup. Use the line you drew to make sure the holes are exactly opposite each other.

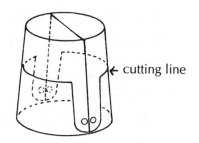

← cutting line

3. Draw tabs around both sets of holes. Cut the cup on the cutting lines as in the drawing (don't cut off the tabs!).

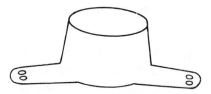

4. Carefully bend out the tabs. Match the holes to holes in the ring base. (If no holes match, just punch a new set in the ring base.) Attach the tabs under the ring base with tab strips.

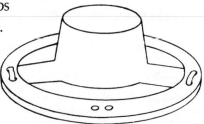

CUPNIK 2

Turn your Cupnik into a satellite—just add a thing or two.

Materials: 1 Cupnik   2 plastic straws
            1 bottle cap   tape   white glue

1. Tape one straw underneath the Cupnik. Tape the other straw so that it crosses the first straw, as in the drawing.

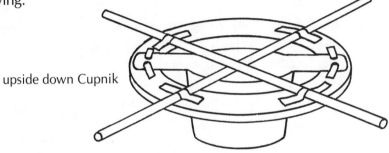

upside down Cupnik

2. Glue the bottle cap on top of the Cupnik.

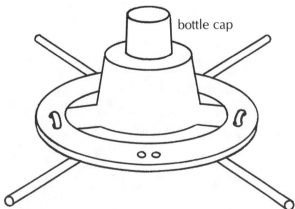

bottle cap

TRIMARAN

Make this even bigger if you like—just use straws to add more rim-and-cup modules.

Materials: 3 cone-shaped plasticware cups   tape
           3 plastic straws   3 large plastic lids

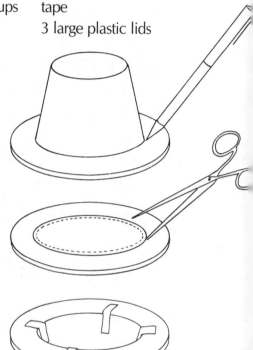

1. Set a cup upside down in the middle of a plastic lid. Trace around the cup. Cut out the lid just *inside* the line. Do the same with the other two lids.

2. Push a cup from the bottom through the middle of a lid. Tape it in four places from underneath. Do the same with the other cups and lids.

make three of these

3. Set the three lids so the edges touch, as in the drawing. Inside the rim of each lid, mark a dot where the rims touch: mark six dots (two on each lid). Punch a hole through each dot.

mark 6 dots altogether

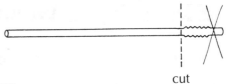

cut

4. Cut the bending edge off a straw and throw it away. On the straight piece you have left, pinch the ends. Fold the flat part and pinch again. Do this to all the straws. (This just makes it easier to push the straws through the holes.)

5. String a straw up through a hole in one lid and down through the hole in another lid. Then push each straw end up through the opposite hole.

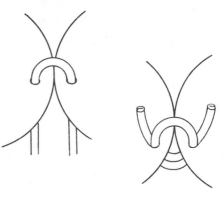

6. Use step 5 to attach the third lid to each of the first two.

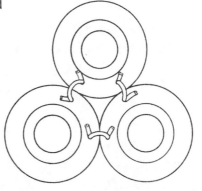

33

WOBBLER

Make an Or-Bit with a weird flight pattern!

Or-Bit parts: 1 ring base   2 tab strips   2 sling wings

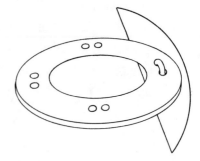

1. Use a tab strip to attach one sling wing under the ring base.

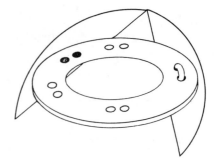

2. Hold the second sling wing under the ring base so it touches the first one. Mark the wing holes on the base. Punch the holes.

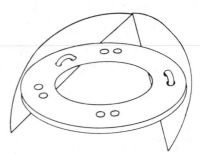

3. Use a tab strip to attach the second sling wing to the new set of holes.

PLATTER SHIPS

Platter Ships are flying flatships—plates, saucers, pizza cardboards, Hula Hoops, even a flying clothesline. With a little know-how, you can send all sorts of strange objects into space. But be sure to give your Platter Ships plastic pizzazz with bright bottle caps, tape, and other wild decorations before they take off (see pages 10–11 for decorating ideas).

PLAIN OLD PLATTER SHIP

Materials: 1 plastic picnicware plate, dinner-size

Most paper and cardboard plates won't fly without a few tricks, but some plastic picnicware plates will. Try a neat wrist flip, and you might just do it.

Cutting the middle out to make it into a ring won't work for plastic plates as it did for plastic lids. Improving its grace in the air, though, is easy. All you need is a Rim Spinner (see next page).

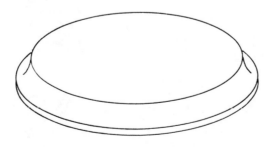

RIM SPINNER

Here's the steadiest flyer in the book—sling it with the tubing *up*!
Tubing can turn any size plastic or cardboard plate, or even a bowl,
into a Rim Spinner.

Materials: 1 plastic or cardboard dinner plate
some plastic aquarium tubing (no wider than your
little finger)
plastic tape

1. Turn the plate upside down. Set the
tubing around the rim of the plate.
Cut the tubing where the ends meet.

2. Tape the tubing into a ring.

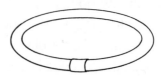

3. Tape the ring inside the rim of an
upside down plate.

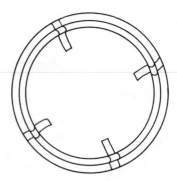

RIM SPINNER 2
(EAT-YOUR-OWN SPACESHIP!)

If you haven't got plastic tubing, make a Rim Spinner with licorice!
And if you haven't got licorice, roll a snake from modeling clay to use
instead. Don't eat the clay, though!

Materials: 1 plastic or cardboard plate or bowl
1 long, fat rope of licorice candy
plastic wrap (from the kitchen)

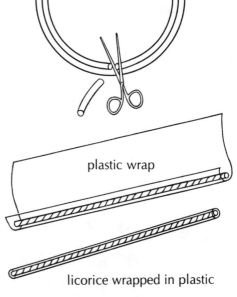

1. Turn the plate upside down. Set the
   licorice around the rim of the plate
   or bowl. Cut it where it meets.

2. Cut off a piece of plastic wrap as
   long as the licorice piece. Tightly
   roll the licorice in the plastic wrap.

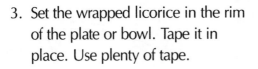

plastic wrap

licorice wrapped in plastic

3. Set the wrapped licorice in the rim
   of the plate or bowl. Tape it in
   place. Use plenty of tape.

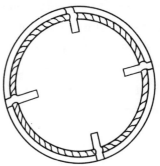

ALLEY-N SHIP

Cut, draw, or paint some windows in this spaceship.

Materials: any Rim Spinner made from a dinner plate
plastic tape   1 picnicware bowl (plastic or cardboard)

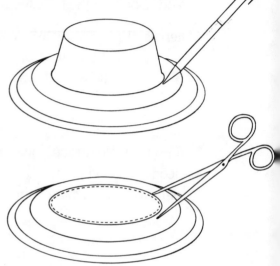

Set the bowl upside down on the middle of the Rim Spinner. Trace around the bowl. Cut *a little inside* the line.

First design:

Push the bowl up through the hole from the bottom. Tape it to the Rim Spinner from underneath.

Second design:

Set the ring upside down on the table. Set the bowl right side up in the middle. Stretch each piece of tape from the bowl rim to the plate rim. (The middle of the tape doesn't stick to anything.) When you turn the spaceship right side up, the bowl will hang underneath!

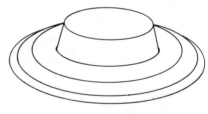

first design

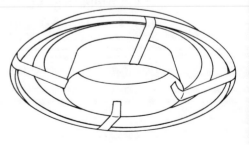

second design

ROPE-A-LOPE

How simple can you get?

Materials: some thick cotton clothesline   1 plastic or paper plate

1. Cut the rim off the plate, leaving a saucer-sized circle (or a little smaller).

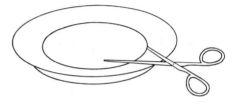

2. Cut a circle out of the center to make a ring shape.

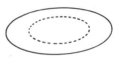

3. Tape one end of the rope to the edge of the circle. Keep taping the rope to the edge all the way around.

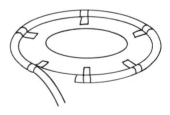

3. Cut the rope so the two ends meet. Tape the ends to the ring.

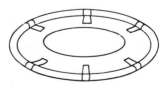

FLAT BRAT

An odd, off-center hole helps the Flat Brat fly. When you add things, balance them—if you glue a cup to one side, glue one to the other side too.

Materials: 1 round pizza cardboard OR
               1 piece of cardboard from the side of a cardboard carton
               1 big dinner plate or round serving platter (to trace around)
               1 saucer or dessert plate (to trace around)

1. Set the biggest plate upside down on the cardboard and trace around it. Cut out the circle. (Skip this step if you have a pizza cardboard.)

2. Set the saucer in the middle of the cardboard circle. Now push it halfway to one edge. Trace around the saucer. Cut out the circle.

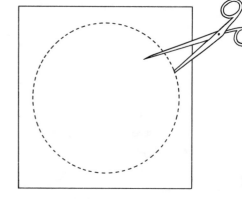

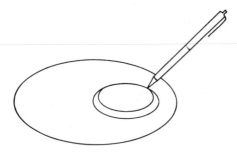

SUPER FLATSHIP

It can be hard to cut through a big carton, so get help with this monster if you need it. Bending down the even sides a little might help this spaceship fly better.

Materials: a BIG cardboard carton   string   pen
          tape   1 sheet of newspaper

1. Tie one end of the string to the pen. Hold the pen at one side of the cardboard piece and stretch the string to the other side. (Do this on the shortest side.)

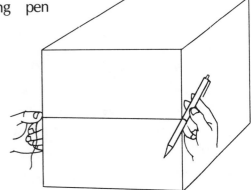

2. Cut the string where it touches the other side of the box. Then cut the string in half.

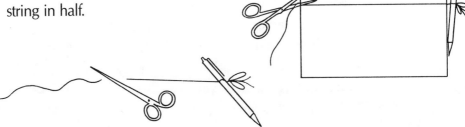

3. Cut one side off the carton. Discard the rest of the box.

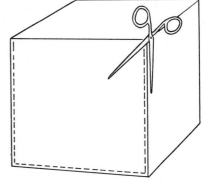

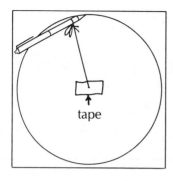

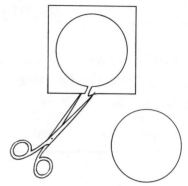

4. Tape one end of the string to the middle of the cardboard piece. Hold down the tape with one hand and stretch the string to draw a circle with the other hand. Cut out the circle.

5. Cut the string in half again. Follow Step 4 to make a smaller circle on a sheet of newspaper.

6. Set the newspaper circle on the cardboard in the center of the circle. Then move the circle halfway to one side, so it looks like the Flat Brat (page 40): side A is twice as wide as side B. Sides C and D are the same.

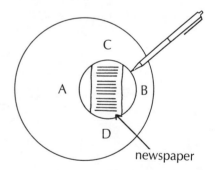

7. Trace around the circle. Cut it out.

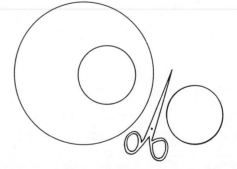

HOOPSHIP

You can fancy up your Hoopship with "Hoop-La" from pages 45-46! (If you can't get vinyl tubing, use an embroidery hoop instead. It's not as big, but it works fine.)

Materials: 3½ feet of stiff vinyl tubing (see page 9 for places to find it)
1 plastic shopping bag (the noisy kind is great!)
OR trash bag
tape

1. Tape the ends of the tubing to make a ring.

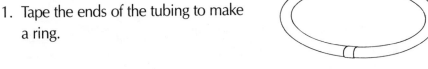

2. Cut open the plastic bag.

3. Lay the ring on the opened bag. Trace around the ring. Then cut out the circle.

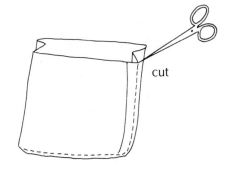

cut

4. Tape the plastic circle to the ring. Follow the steps on the next page so your Hoopship is nice and tight.

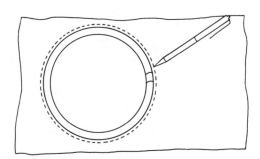

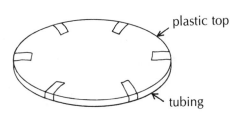

plastic top

tubing

How to Tape a Plastic Circle to a Hoop

1. Cut eight pieces of tape about as long as your little finger (2 inches). Stick them up in a handy place.

2. Stick tape #1 to the circle. Stick tape #2 on the opposite side.

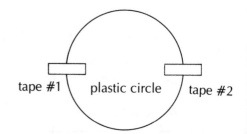

tape #1   plastic circle   tape #2

3. Hold the circle with a piece of tape in each hand. Stretch it *gently* over the hoop and tape it to the hoop. (If you pull too hard, you won't have a circle!)

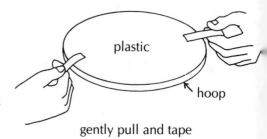

plastic

hoop

gently pull and tape

4. Stick tapes #3 and #4 to the plastic top. Now pull gently with both hands and stick the tape to the hoop. The top should be getting nice and tight.

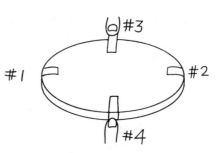

#3

#1   #2

#4

5. Follow Step 4 to stick on tape pieces #5 and #6. Do it again with #7 and #8.

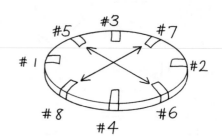

#5   #3   #7

#1   #2

#8   #4   #6

HOOP-LA

Make a Hoopship and then add some excitement. Here are some ideas to get you started.

Cut a hole in the middle of the Hoopship, making a ring.

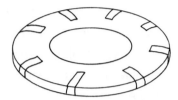

Draw a spiral pattern on your Hoopship. Or stick plastic caps all over it.

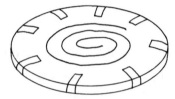

Cut a small hole in the middle. Then draw a big circle around the hole. Make a fringe by cutting to the drawn circle all the way around. It makes *noise* when you fly it.!

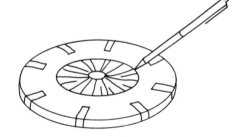

cut on the lines to drawn circle

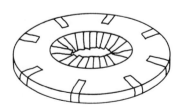

45

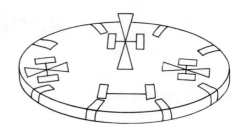

Cut a rubber band open. Stretch it a little and tape it to the plastic top. Park a small spaceship under the rubber band. If you make more than one parking place, space them evenly, so the Hoopship will still fly.

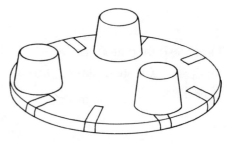

Tape see-through plastic cone cups to the plastic top. Put things in them and give them a ride.

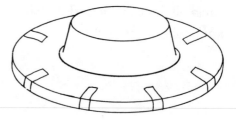

Or tape a picnicware bowl or plate to the center.

HURLA HOOP

Try making a giant space station! Add anything you like from pages 45-46 (but don't cut a hole in a middle). To fly your Hurla Hoop, use both hands to fling it gently, like a giant Frisbee. (If you can't find a Hula Hoop, make your own with 7 feet of stiff vinyl tubing, page 9. Just tape the ends together.)

Materials: 1 Hula Hoop   tape
          1 large plastic trash bag

1. Cut the trash bag and open it up.

2. Lay the Hula Hoop on the opened bag. Trace around it. Cut out the circle.

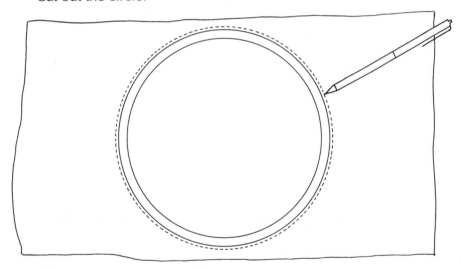

3. Tape the circle to the Hula Hoop, following the steps on page 44.

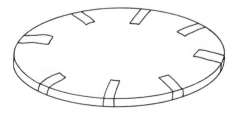